HOW MACHINES WORK

FAST CARS

IAN GRAHAM

A+

Smart Apple Media

Smart Apple Media is published by Black Rabbit Books
P.O. Box 3263, Mankato, Minnesota 56002

Printed in Hong Kong

Library of Congress Cataloging-in-Publication Data

Graham, Ian, 1953–
    Fast cars / Ian Graham.
    p. cm.—(Smart Apple Media—how machines work)
    Includes index.
    Summary: "Describes in detail how high-performance sports cars and supercars are designed to drive faster than average cars"—Provided by publisher.
    ISBN 978-1-59920-289-1
    1. Automobiles, Racing—Design and construction—Juvenile literature. I. Title.
TL236.G665 2009
629.222'1—dc22

2008002402

Created by Q2AMedia
Series Editor: Honor Head
Book Editor: Harriet McGregor
Senior Art Director: Ashita Murgai
Designers: Harleen Mehta, Ravijot Singh
Picture Researcher: Amit Tigga

All words in **bold** can be found in Glossary on pages 30–31.

Web site information is correct at time of going to press. However, the publishers cannot accept liability for any information or links found on third-party Web sites.

Picture credits
t=top b=bottom c=center l=left r=right m=middle
Cover Images: Main Image: BMW AG. Smaller Image tl: Porsche

Bugatti: 4, BMW: 5t, Mazda: 5b, Ferrari: 6, Mark Scheuern/ Alamy: 6 inset, Porsche: 8, 9t, Daimlerchrysler: 10, 11t, BMW: 11b, Bugatti: 12, Transtock Inc./ Alamy: 13t, BMW: 13b, Graham Harrison/ Alamy: 14, Goodyear: 15, Ford: 16t, BMW: 16b, Porche: 18t, Chris Alan Wilton/ Gettyimages: 18b, Porche: 19, Johannes Flex/ Shutterstock: 20, Motoring Picture Library/ Alamy: 21t, Michael Shake/ Bigstockphoto: 21b, Daimlerchrysler: 22, Ford: 23, 25tr, 25ml, Transtock Inc./ Alamy: 25br, Mazda Automobiles: 26, NMGB: 27, 27 inset, Car Culture/ Corbis: 28t, SAAB Automobiles: 28b, Mark Scheuern/ Alamy: 29t, Mazda Automobiles: 29b

Q2AMedia Art Bank: 7, 9b, 17, 24b

9 8 7 6 5 4 3 2 1

CONTENTS

FAST CARS

Fast cars are designed to be more fun to drive than ordinary cars. Their size, weight, power, and shape give them great performance on the road.

HOW FAST IS A FAST CAR?

The fastest cars on the roads have a top speed of about 250 mph (400 km/h), but a very high top speed is not all-important in a road car. A car that goes fast in a straight line may not be very good at cornering. Fast road cars have to be all-arounders. In addition to being fast, they have to **accelerate**, corner, and stop quickly, too.

▼ The Bugatti Veyron is the world's fastest production car—and one of the most expensive!

BUGATTI VEYRON 16.4

Specification

Engine:	8.0 l W16 turbocharged
Power:	1,001 hp (746 kW)
Acceleration:	0–62 mph (0–100 km/h) in 2.5 seconds
Top speed:	253 mph (407 km/h)

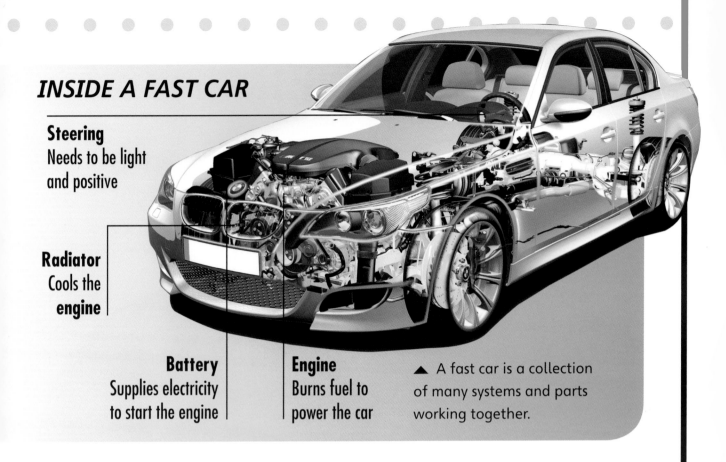

INSIDE A FAST CAR

Steering
Needs to be light
and positive

Radiator
Cools the
engine

Battery
Supplies electricity
to start the engine

Engine
Burns fuel to
power the car

▲ A fast car is a collection
of many systems and parts
working together.

SPORTS AND SUPERS

There are two main types of fast road cars. Sports cars are
small and light. Most sports cars have only two seats because
they are shorter than other cars. Being short and light
allows them to make tight turns faster. Many sports cars are
convertibles—their roof can be taken off or folded back.

Supercars are even faster. They have bigger, more powerful
engines, and they look fantastic, too!

◀ The Mazda MX5 Miata is a classic
two-seater sports car. It is small, light
and close to the ground.

A NOTE ABOUT SPEED
Fast cars are designed for
speed, but also for safety.
Even supercars MUST
obey the speed limit!

ENGINE POWER

Fast cars depend on the design of their engines for their power and speed. The styling and weight of the cars also add to their fantastic performance.

▼ The powerful 8-cylinder engine and smooth lines of this Ferrari F430 make it one of today's top-performing supercars.

FERRARI F430

Specification

Engine: 4.3 l V8
Power: 490 hp (365 kW)
Acceleration: 0–62 mph (0–100 km/h)
                  in 4.0 seconds
Top speed: 196 mph (315 kph)

HOW AN ENGINE WORKS

A car's engine produces the power to turn the wheels. Some fast cars have very big engines, but a big engine is not always needed. A small engine may be powerful enough for a small, light car. Inside the engine, explosions are caused by burning **fuel** in bottle-shaped **cylinders**. The explosions make **pistons** move up and down inside the cylinders. The up and down movements of the pistons make the car's wheels turn.

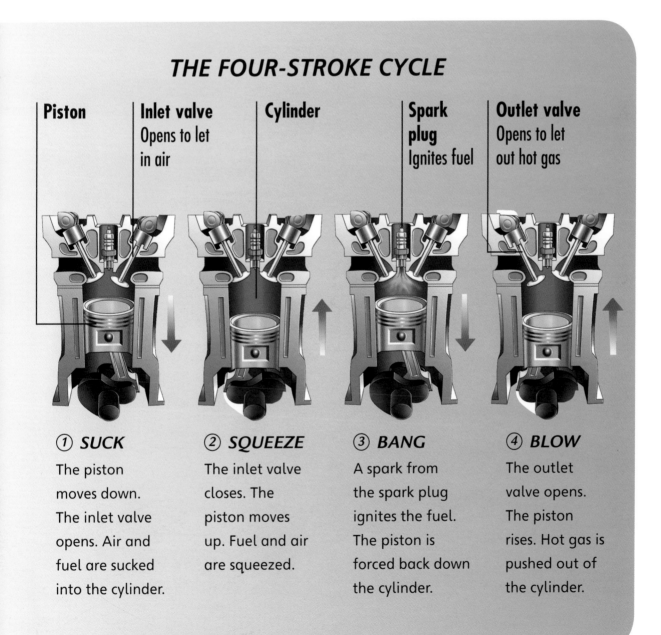

THE FOUR-STROKE CYCLE

Piston

Inlet valve Opens to let in air

Cylinder

Spark plug Ignites fuel

Outlet valve Opens to let out hot gas

① *SUCK*
The piston moves down. The inlet valve opens. Air and fuel are sucked into the cylinder.

② *SQUEEZE*
The inlet valve closes. The piston moves up. Fuel and air are squeezed.

③ *BANG*
A spark from the spark plug ignites the fuel. The piston is forced back down the cylinder.

④ *BLOW*
The outlet valve opens. The piston rises. Hot gas is pushed out of the cylinder.

WHERE'S THE ENGINE?

When a car is designed, the engine is chosen to match its size, weight, and speed. Most cars have their engine at the front, but the fastest cars often have their engine in the middle, behind the driver. The engine is the heaviest part of a car. Putting it in the middle spreads out its weight more evenly between the wheels.

A car engine is a complicated machine with hundreds of moving parts. Slippery oil keeps them moving easily.

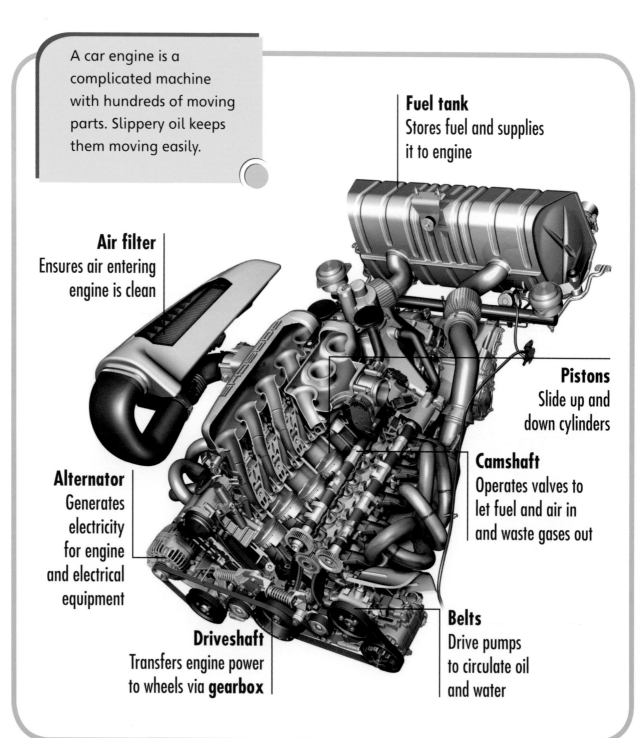

Fuel tank
Stores fuel and supplies it to engine

Air filter
Ensures air entering engine is clean

Pistons
Slide up and down cylinders

Camshaft
Operates valves to let fuel and air in and waste gases out

Alternator
Generates electricity for engine and electrical equipment

Driveshaft
Transfers engine power to wheels via **gearbox**

Belts
Drive pumps to circulate oil and water

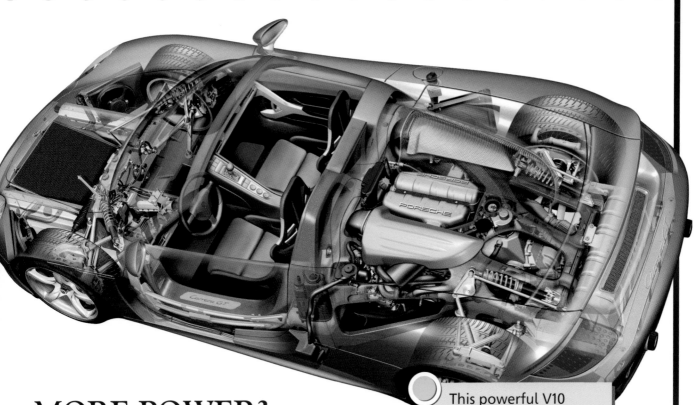

MORE POWER?

Most car engines burn gasoline, but the fastest racing cars use a rocket fuel called nitromethane. If a car needs more power, it can be given an engine with more, or bigger, cylinders. Adding a turbocharger produces even more power. It pushes extra air into the engine so it can burn fuel even faster.

This powerful V10 engine can take the Porsche Carrera GT from 0 to 124 mph (0–200 kp/h) in under 10 seconds.

▶ Inside the turbocharger, exhaust gases from the car's engine drive a turbine which is linked to a compressor unit. The compressor sucks in extra air and forces it into the engine cylinders.

① Exhaust gases from engine drive turbine

② Turbine drives compressor

③ Compressor sucks in fresh air and forces it into engine

Turbine and compressor mounted on shared **axle**

THE POWER TRAIN

The huge power of a fast car's engine is sent to its wheels by a series of parts called the **power train**. This includes the **clutch**, the gearbox, and the **differential**.

▼ A car's power train carries the engine's power to the wheels.

MERCEDES SLK 55 AMG

Specification

Engine:	5.4 l V8
Power:	360 hp (268 kW)
Acceleration:	0–62 mph (0–100 km/h) in 4.9 seconds
Top speed:	155 mph (250 kph)

HOW THE POWER TRAIN WORKS

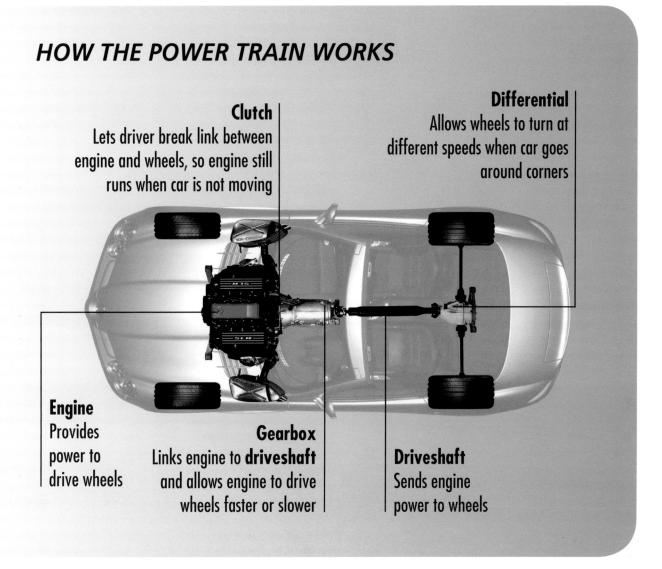

Clutch
Lets driver break link between engine and wheels, so engine still runs when car is not moving

Differential
Allows wheels to turn at different speeds when car goes around corners

Engine
Provides power to drive wheels

Gearbox
Links engine to **driveshaft** and allows engine to drive wheels faster or slower

Driveshaft
Sends engine power to wheels

GOING FASTER

A driver makes a car go faster by pressing the **accelerator**. This sends more fuel to the engine. To go even faster, the driver has to change **gears**. The gears are toothed wheels that interlock. When one gear turns, it turns the next gear. By choosing different gears to link the engine to the wheels, the driver can make the car go faster or slower.

▲ To go at different speeds, the driver changes gears by moving the gear stick. A car can have up to six gears, including a reverse gear for going backward.

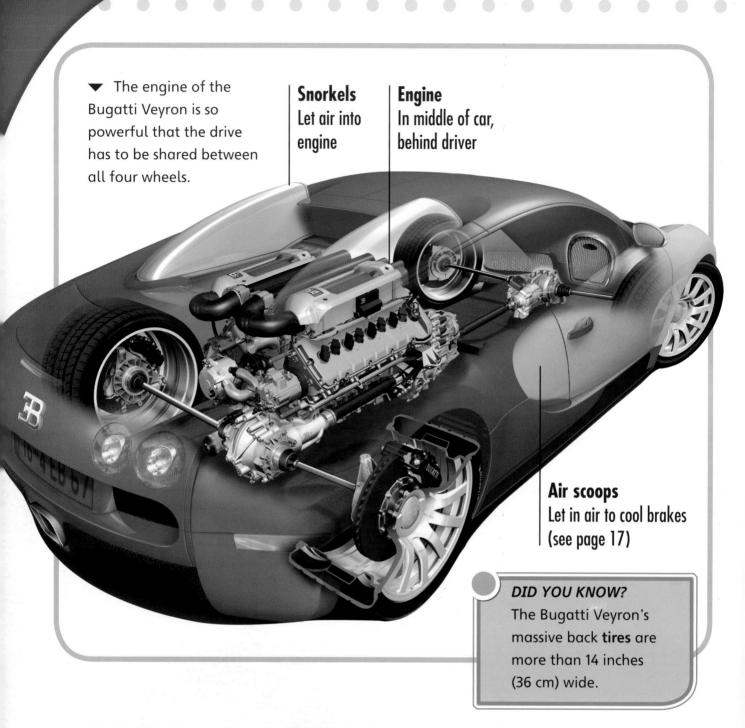

▼ The engine of the Bugatti Veyron is so powerful that the drive has to be shared between all four wheels.

Snorkels
Let air into engine

Engine
In middle of car, behind driver

Air scoops
Let in air to cool brakes (see page 17)

> **DID YOU KNOW?**
> The Bugatti Veyron's massive back **tires** are more than 14 inches (36 cm) wide.

DRIVING THE WHEELS

Most fast car engines drive only two of the car's four wheels. A few supercars have engines so powerful that two wheels are not able to handle all the power. These cars have all-wheel drive. All four wheels are driven by the engine. Only the most powerful supercars use all-wheel drive because the parts add extra weight to the car.

LAMBORGHINI MURCIELAGO LP640

Specification

Engine: 6.5 l V12
Power: 640 hp (471kW)
Acceleration: 0–62 mph (0–100 km/h) in 3.4 seconds
Top speed: 210 mph (340 km/h)

▼ The all-wheel-drive
Lamborghini Murcielago

AUTOMATIC AND MANUAL

In a car with an **automatic transmission**, the gear changes automatically as the driver accelerates or decelerates. In other cars, the driver changes gear by moving a gear stick. Instead of a gear stick, some fast cars have switches called **paddles** on the steering wheel. Pressing one paddle makes the car go up a gear. Pressing the other paddle makes the car go down a gear.

▶ The steering wheel of the BMW M5 has paddle switches for changing gears.

Paddle switches

WHEELS AND TIRES

A car's tires have two important jobs. They support the weight of the car and they use engine power to move the car.

HOW TIRES WORK

A car's tires are made of air-filled rubber. Tires are made of rubber because this soft material grips the road well. If water gets between the tires and the road, it stops the tires from gripping. The car will **skid** and the driver will not be able to steer or **brake**. The zigzag grooves in a car's tires are called the **tread**. On a wet surface, the tread allows water to be squeezed out from under the tire.

▼ Car tires need to grip the road, even when the surface is covered with water.

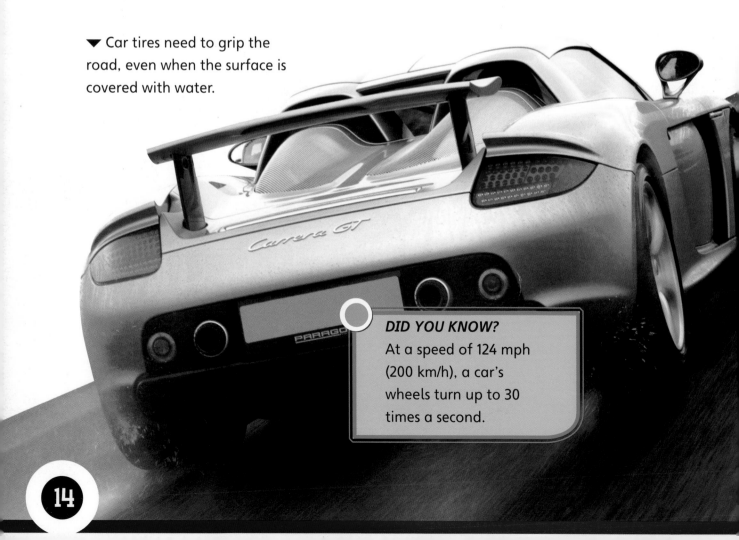

DID YOU KNOW?
At a speed of 124 mph (200 km/h), a car's wheels turn up to 30 times a second.

INSIDE A TIRE

Cap plies
Hold other
layers in place

Body plies
Made of fabric
covered with rubber

Tread
Made from natural
and man-made
rubber

Sidewall
Protects body
plies and
stops air from
escaping

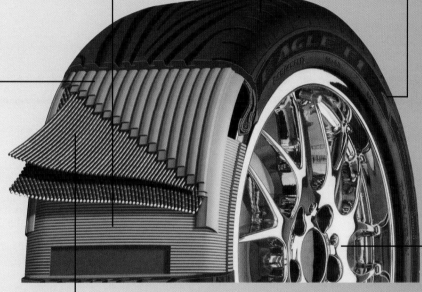

Metal rim
Bolted to axle
of car

Steel belts
Strengthen area
beneath tread

▲ Fabric, steel, and rubber give a tire the
right amount of strength and flexibility.

▶ A car tire fits
tightly into grooves
around the metal
rim of the wheel.

SUSPENSION

A car's wheels are linked to the rest of the car by sets of springs. These springy links are called the **suspension** system. They let the wheels move up and down over bumps in the ground, while the rest of the car moves along more smoothly. The air-filled tires help to cushion the car from small bumps, too.

Coil spring
Squashes up and springs back as wheels go over bumps

Steering link
Connects wheel to steering system

▼ The coiled springs of a car's suspension system give a smooth ride for the driver and passengers.

DID YOU KNOW?
An average driver uses a car's brakes about 75,000 times a year.

HOW DO CARS STOP?

A driver slows a car by pressing the brake pedal. This makes a pair of tough pads squeeze together and grip a disc, which is attached to the wheel and turns with it. Gripping the disc slows the wheel down, which slows down the whole car. This type of brake is called a **disc brake**.

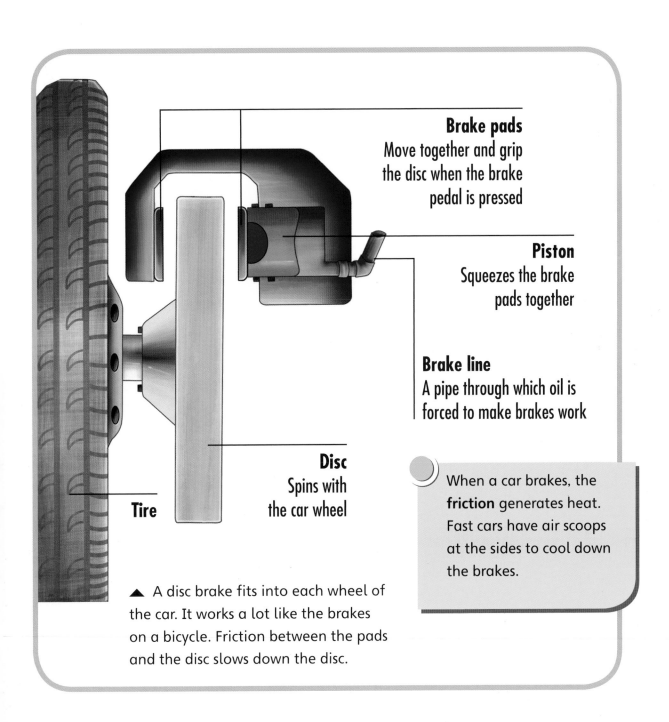

Brake pads
Move together and grip the disc when the brake pedal is pressed

Piston
Squeezes the brake pads together

Brake line
A pipe through which oil is forced to make brakes work

Disc
Spins with the car wheel

Tire

When a car brakes, the **friction** generates heat. Fast cars have air scoops at the sides to cool down the brakes.

▲ A disc brake fits into each wheel of the car. It works a lot like the brakes on a bicycle. Friction between the pads and the disc slows down the disc.

SHAPE AND BUILD

A fast car has a low, smooth, gently curving shape so that air can easily flow around it. This helps it go as fast as possible. It also uses less fuel.

SHAPED FOR SPEED

When a fast car moves through the air, the air pushes back. If a car is the wrong shape, the air pushes back and slows it down. This is called air **resistance**, or **drag**. If a car is the right shape, air easily flows around it and the car can go much faster.

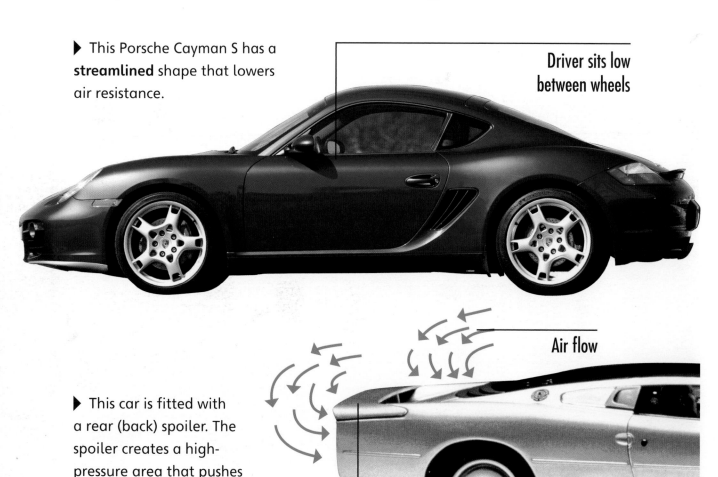

▶ This Porsche Cayman S has a **streamlined** shape that lowers air resistance.

Driver sits low between wheels

Air flow

▶ This car is fitted with a rear (back) spoiler. The spoiler creates a high-pressure area that pushes down on the rear of the car. This helps it go faster.

Spoiler

THE WIND TUNNEL TEST

The shape of a fast car is tested in a **wind tunnel**. A car, or a model of it, is placed inside the tunnel. Air is then blown through the tunnel. The way the air flows around the car is measured. One way to see how air flows around a car in a wind tunnel is to use smoke. The flowing air is invisible, but streams of smoke blowing with the air can be seen by the human eye.

▼ Smoke shows how air flows around a car in a wind tunnel test.

DID YOU KNOW?
Wind tunnels have been used to test the shape of vehicles since the 1890s.

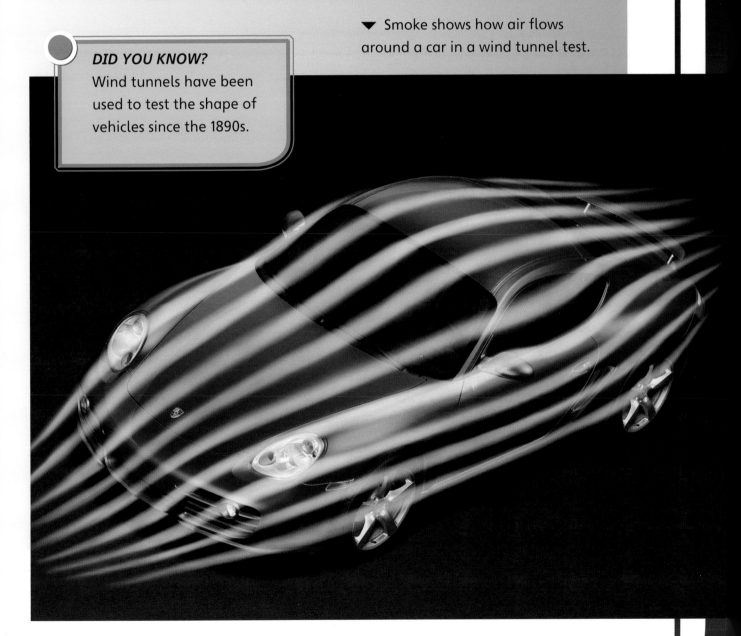

WHAT ARE CARS MADE OF?

Most cars are made of steel, a strong metal that can be bent into any shape. Because steel is heavy, some parts of a car are made from lighter metals, such as aluminum, to reduce the weight. Aluminum is only one-third as strong as steel, but it is much lighter and does not rust.

BMW Z4 COUPE 3.0si SPORT

Specification

Engine:	3.0 l inline 6
Power:	265 hp (197 kW)
Acceleration:	0–62 mph (0–100 km/h) in 5.7 seconds
Top speed:	155 mph (250 kph)

Windshield
Made of safety glass

Hood
Made of aluminum to save weight

▲ The BMW Z4 sports car is a superb example of precision engineering.

Body
Made of steel for strength

Tough metallic paint finish
Protects steel body against rust

CARBON CARS

The fastest cars are often made from materials that are lighter than steel. Some sports cars have a body made of plastic. Supercars are often made from a material called **carbon fiber**. To make a carbon-fiber part for a car, mats of woven carbon fibers are laid in a mold and soaked in liquid plastic, which dries hard. This material is very strong and light.

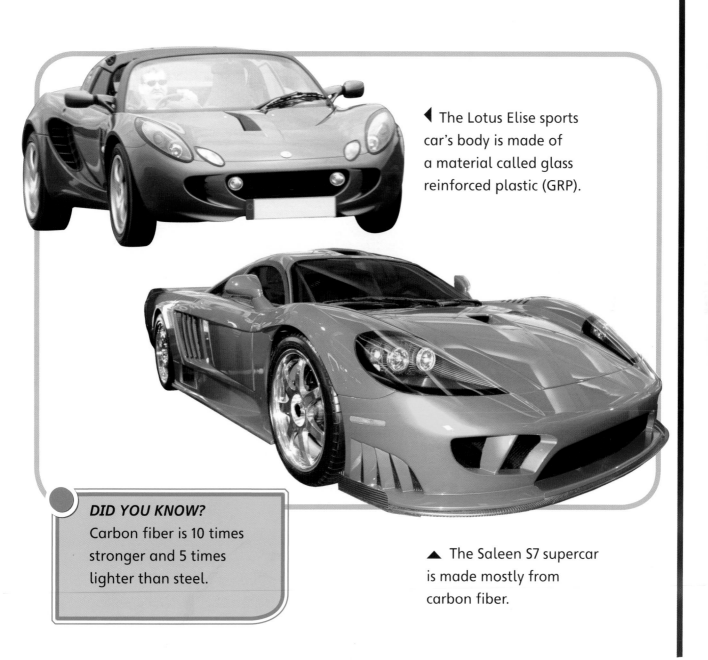

◀ The Lotus Elise sports car's body is made of a material called glass reinforced plastic (GRP).

DID YOU KNOW?
Carbon fiber is 10 times stronger and 5 times lighter than steel.

▲ The Saleen S7 supercar is made mostly from carbon fiber.

SAFETY FIRST

Fast cars are exciting to drive and are designed to be safe at high speeds. They have built-in safety features to protect the driver and passengers.

▼ Safety features of a fast car

Air bag
Blows up like a balloon when car crashes

Soft materials
Cushion and protect passengers

Safety glass
Reduces risk of injury if windshield shatters

Seatbelts
Hold driver and passengers safely in seats

Many fast cars have airbags in the front, as well as side bags for extra protection.

SAFE DESIGN

If a fast-moving car is involved in a crash, seatbelts protect the driver and passengers by holding them safely in their seats. They also spread the impact of a crash over a person's entire body, so there is less risk of injury.

▼ The part of a fast car where the driver and passengers sit is made extra-strong for safety.

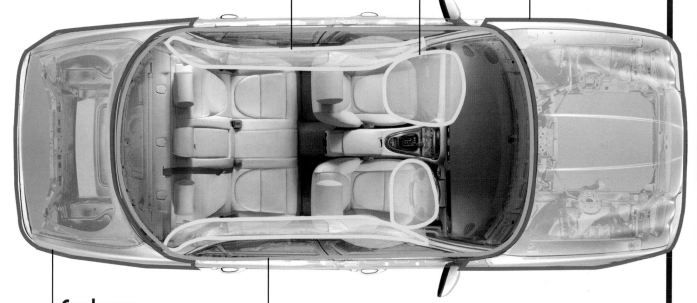

Side and front air bags
Blow up instantly if car is in a crash

Crush zone

Crush zone
Crumples first in collision to absorb impact

Safety cell
Strengthened to protect driver and passengers

SUPERCAR SAFETY

The fastest road cars have some of the same safety features as race cars. In case of a serious crash, a race car driver sits inside a super-strong tub called a **safety cell**. The fastest road cars have a safety cell, too. Other parts of the car at the front and back are made weaker than the safety cell. In a crash, these weaker parts are designed to crumple first to protect the driver and passengers.

HOW AN AIR BAG WORKS

When a car hits something, air bags instantly blow up like balloons inside the car to protect the driver and passengers. The car measures how fast the car stops and can tell the difference between braking hard and a crash. If it decides the car is in a crash, it sets off a device that releases a lot of gas very quickly. This blows up the air bag, which acts like a cushion.

◀ In a collision, the air bag instantly inflates, protecting the driver's head from injury.

DID YOU KNOW?
A car air bag blows up in 0.8 seconds—faster than the blink of an eye!

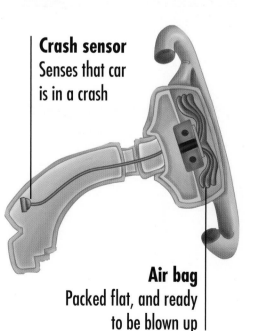

Crash sensor
Senses that car is in a crash

Air bag
Packed flat, and ready to be blown up

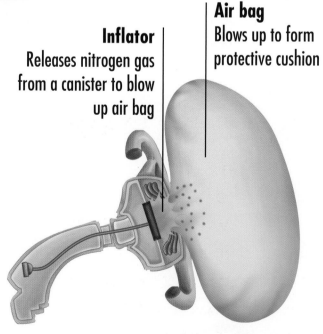

Inflator
Releases nitrogen gas from a canister to blow up air bag

Air bag
Blows up to form protective cushion

TESTING FOR SAFETY

In safety tests, **crash test dummies** sit in the cars. The dummies are built like people. Their movements and the forces acting on them are measured to find out what would happen to people in a real crash.

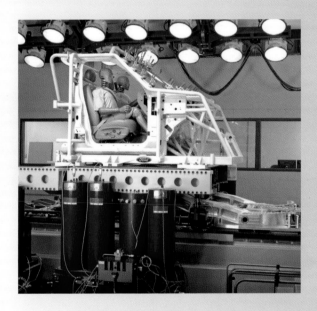

▲ "Dummies" are used in a specially designed **crash simulator** to see what would happen in a real car crash.

◀ The effects of a real car crash are tested on dummies in a **crash simulator**.

SPOT THE CAMERA!

If the engine is at the back of a car, it can be hard for the driver to see behind when backing up. In addition to the normal mirrors, the Saleen S7 supercar has a camera in the back which sends a picture to a screen in the car. Can you find the camera?

Answer: just above the space between the "L" and the "E" of "SALEEN".

FUTURE CARS

The cars of the future are already being designed today! New ideas that may be used in the future are tested by building vehicles called **concept cars**.

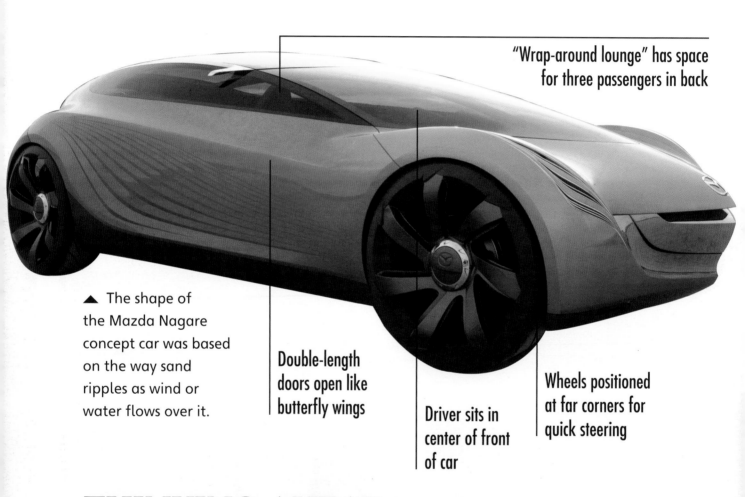

"Wrap-around lounge" has space for three passengers in back

▲ The shape of the Mazda Nagare concept car was based on the way sand ripples as wind or water flows over it.

Double-length doors open like butterfly wings

Driver sits in center of front of car

Wheels positioned at far corners for quick steering

THINKING AHEAD

Concept cars are not built in large numbers and cannot be bought by the public. They are experimental cars. Many of them cannot even be driven because they have no engine. They are put on display at motor shows around the world to see what people think of them. If the ideas tested in a concept car turn out to be popular, they may be built into future cars.

INSIDE A CONCEPT CAR

Designers of concept cars often like to play with new ideas. Why not have the controls operated by the driver's voice instead of switches? Why not have instruments that talk to the driver instead of the driver having to look at them? Why not put the driver's seat in the middle of the car instead of one side?

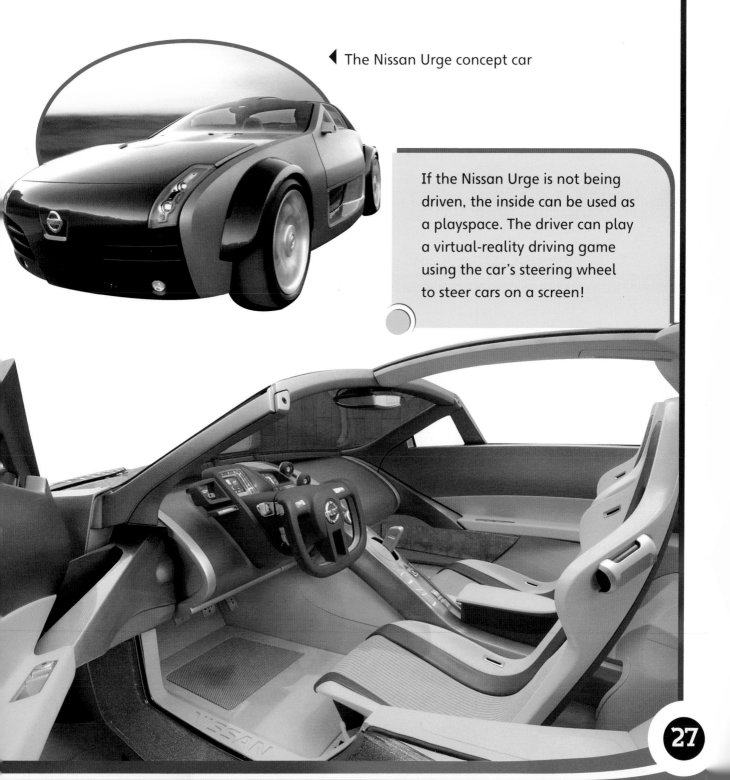

◀ The Nissan Urge concept car

If the Nissan Urge is not being driven, the inside can be used as a playspace. The driver can play a virtual-reality driving game using the car's steering wheel to steer cars on a screen!

IS IT A CAR? IS IT A PLANE?

Designers of concept cars sometimes use materials and shapes borrowed from other types of vehicles—especially aircraft. Planes and cars are alike in some ways. Although planes fly and cars move along the ground, they both travel through the air and they both have to be steered. The insides of some concept cars look very much like aircraft cockpits.

Curved windshield gives driver full 180-degree vision

▼ The roof, windshield, and sides of the Saab Aero-X are made in one piece, like a jet-fighter's cockpit cover.

▼ The dashboard of the Saab Aero-X displays information on glowing screens.

GULL-WING AND SCISSOR DOORS

Instead of opening in the usual way, some concept cars have doors that slide open sideways or lift upward. Car doors that swing upward are known as gull-wing doors because they look like a bird's wings. Sometimes there are no doors at all because the whole top of the car opens up.

▶ This Ford Mustang concept car's doors are called scissor doors because of the way they open.

DID YOU KNOW?
The Alfa Romeo Spix is a concept car that is designed to fly!

◀ The gull-wing doors of the Mazda Ryuga allow both sides of the car to swing open.

GLOSSARY

Accelerate
To go faster

Accelerator A pedal that is pressed to make a car go faster

Air bag A safety device that blows up to protect the driver or passenger

Air resistance When air pushes back against a moving car

Alternator A part of a car that supplies electricity for the engine and equipment

Automatic transmission A type of transmission that changes gear on its own

Axle The metal rod on which wheels are fixed

Battery The part that supplies electricity to a motor

Brake To slow down a car; the part that slows or stops the car

Carbon fiber A strong, light material used to make some fast cars

Clutch The part that allows the driver to break the link between the engine and wheels

Concept car An experimental car built to show or test new ideas

Crash simulator Machine for testing what happens in a real car crash

Crash test dummy A model used to test how safe a car is

Cylinder The part of a car engine where fuel is burned

Differential A set of gears that lets the wheels turn at different speeds when a car goes around a corner

Disc brake A type of brake where pads are squeezed together to slow down the wheel

Drag See **Air resistance**

Driveshaft A metal bar that carries a car's engine power to its wheels

Engine The machine that burns fuel to provide the power needed to make a car move

Friction The effect produced when one surface rubs against another

Fuel Liquid burned in a car's engine to provide power

Gear A toothed wheel

Gearbox A set of gears that allow the engine to drive the wheels at different speeds

Paddles Gear switches on the steering wheel

Piston The part of a car engine that is forced up and down inside a cylinder

Power train The parts of a car that link the engine to the wheels

Radiator The part that helps to cool a car's engine by letting heat escape

Safety cell The strong part of a car built to protect people in a crash

Skid To slide out of control

Snorkel A tube through which air passes

Streamlined Shaped so that air flows around easily

Supercar A very fast, high-performance road car

Suspension The springy links between the wheels and the rest of the car

Tire The air-filled rubber tube around a car's wheel

Tread The grooves in a car's tires

Wind tunnel Equipment for studying how a car's shape affects air resistance

INDEX

Web Sites

For Kids:

http://www.learn4good.com/games/cars/auto_racing.htm

http://www.learn4good.com/games/cars/the_fast_and_the_
    furious_street_racer.htm

For Teachers:

http://www.sportscarcup.com/concept-cars

http://auto.howstuffworks.com/bugatti.htm